Articulate Better with Speech Therapy

26 Effective Speech Therapy Strategies for Children and Adults to Articulate Better in 20 days

Table of Contents

Introduction

Speech Therapy can help both kids and adults who have an articulation problem or who stutter a lot. There are many other reasons for speech therapy and many people suffer from it due to genetic disorders or organ failure.

Teaching speech therapy to kids can be difficult because they lack an understanding of what is happening to them. These kids require special attention and, hence, this book will teach you how you can get your kid to indulge in activities that will help make them speak better. These activities are simple and their aim is to identify and slowly solve the problem that is causing articulation issues.

Adults can also easily develop speech related problems – either they can have disorders that have gone untreated since birth or some accident/body impairment can cause it. Most of the speech related problems in adults are caused by larger medical conditions such as blood clotting in the brain or vocal injury. These can be treated as well with the help of the right strategies that have been listed in this book.

If you want to start with speech therapy, then you should have a goal in your mind. This will help you to stay motivated and you'll strive to work harder. Speech therapy can be frustrating sometimes because it can take a lot of time, but you have to believe in yourself and you'll eventually see the results.

Chapter 1: Overview of Speech Problems

It's imperative that you understand articulation or phonological disorder because this will aid in the rehabilitation process. It's important to note that young children will naturally incur difficulties when learning how to speak but, as they grow older, they should be able to overcome these phonological difficulties and articulate properly. If you're an adult who still has these problems then it's imperative that you learn to identify your problem before you start on the recovery path.

What are speech problems? Speech problems are conditions characterized by the inability of an individual to pronounce words properly and express himself. It is usually caused by an abnormal functioning of the brain. It's a learning disability that can impede learning progress.

Types of Articulation Disorders

There are four types of articulation errors that people make – Substitutions, Omissions, Distortions and Additions.

Substitution:

It means replacing one sound with another sound. Example – wed for read or thoap for soap.

Omissions:

Omitting a sound in a word. Example – p_ay the piano for play the piano or g_ee _nake for green snake.

Distortions:

Producing a sound in an unfamiliar way. Example – pencil (nasal sound – like an m) for pencil.

Additions:

Inserting an extra sound within a word. Example – buhlack horse for black horse or doguh for dog.

Diagnosis

What are the causes for speech problems? There are a number of causes related to speech problems. Most of them are other serious disorders that have manifested themselves through speech disorders. Below are some of the conditions that may cause speech disorders:

Autism or Autism Spectrum Disorder (ASD)

This is a developmental disorder in which people have a delayed development of their social skills, language and behavior. It starts from an early age and is mostly observed in children and continues to impact them even when they are adults.

Observe your child and notice how he interacts with other people. Is he unable to socialize with kids of his own age? Does he have difficulty speaking? Does he isolate himself from the rest of the group? If you have answered "Yes" to any of these questions, then you should consult a specialist to establish whether your child indeed has ASD. This will help in controlling the problem now so that it doesn't have devastating consequences in the future.

Apraxia

This is also known as Childhood Apraxia of Speech (CAS) and is characterized by a child's inability to say the word because his brain and his muscle movements are not in congruence with each other. In this motor-speech disorder, your child may have difficulties pronouncing long syllables and may tend to shorten or miss syllables that are difficult to pronounce. He knows what to say but he cannot articulate well. An example is when he says "bana" instead of "banana", or "flor" rather than "flower."

Intellectual disability

This disability is characterized by mental impedance. This denotes that the speech problem occurs because the child has delayed development in all aspects of his life. Understandably, his learning progress will be slower than kids of his age, and that's why he cannot articulate well. The primary aspect of mental impedance is that the child cannot understand simple instructions and has poor memory.

Neurological conditions

These are conditions that affect the nerves and the brain, such as cerebral palsy, muscular dystrophy and similar brain disorders. All of these can cause problems in articulation and cause phonological disorders. This can also happen as a result of accidents, brain injury or trauma and even extreme shock.

Auditory Processing Disorder (APD)

This involves the ability of the Central Nervous System (CNS) to interpret auditory information. There are various conditions affecting this process, such as Attention Deficit Hyperactivity Disorder (ADHD), autism, and environmental conditions (noisy surroundings). There are also cases in which the hearing organs are dysfunctional, sending the wrong messages to the CNS.

The CNS processes all stimuli transmitted by the different parts of the body and when these nerve signals are misinterpreted, proper speech and articulation can be difficult to attain. The brain may also confuse the phonology of words, so the person won't be able to say the words correctly.

Selective Mutism

This is a disorder where a person remains silent in certain situations. In this condition, he can selectively choose when to remain silent. An example is when a child—who is afraid of his father—remains silent when his father is around him. Another example is when a student refuses to speak when in school because of the fear of committing a grammatical error and being ostracized.

Hearing loss

You may be unaware of it but your child may not be able to hear, that's why he doesn't speak, and when he does, his speech is unintelligible. You have to determine that your child is not deaf before dealing with his speech problems. A simple hearing test will suffice.

Steps for the simple hearing test:

1. Let your child sit in the center of a room.

2. Instruct him to close his eyes.

3. Prepare two coins, and position yourself in front of him, staying several feet away.

4. Hold the coins with your fingers and click them against each other.

5. Continue clicking and ask him to identify your location.

6. Proceed to his right side and click the coins again.

7. Let him identify your location.

8. Go to his left side and click the coins anew.

9. Let him identify your position.

10. If he has no hearing defect, he should be able to identify all your positions correctly.

11. If he fails to do so, observe the ear that has committed the error and write down your observations.

12. You'll have to consult your Eye, Ear, Nose and Throat (EENT) specialist if you suspect that he has a hearing disorder. The EENT will begin treatment, once the cause of the hearing loss is determined.

If your child has no signs of hearing loss, then you can proceed to implement the steps provided in this book.

Defects of speech organs

There may also be defects with his palate or vocal chords. You can consult your physician and rule out aural or oral defects before proceeding with your therapeutic exercises. They will conduct a physical examination of the oral cavity and observe for vocal cord injuries or palate impairment.

Once you have determined the cause of your or your child's speech problems, you can now start to rehabilitate his speech and use interventions that can develop his articulation and phonology.

Chapter 2: Strategies for Children

Resolving speech problems can take longer if you delay therapy after your child has been diagnosed. Doing home activities is convenient for you and your child, and will also be tremendously helpful in improving your child's speech. It's also easier to conduct speech therapy at home because children tend to perform better when they work in an environment that they trust.

Here are some home activities that can help your child:

Bonding activities

These are activities that allow you to openly express love and concern for your child. Therapy can only be effective when your child is self-motivated. His self-motivation can stem from his knowledge that no matter what, he's still loved. He should feel that he belongs and that he's loved unconditionally. Your bonding activities can involve family outings or picnics, traveling to scenic places or simple heart-to-heart conversations.

Your child needs your love to be able to accomplish great things, so you must express your love verbally and through your actions. Family members should also openly express their support for the member of the family with speech problems. He must never be laughed at, ridiculed or ostracized because of his speech disorder. When he feels confident and secure about himself, he will have the confidence to speak more clearly and emphatically.

During these bonding events, you can play fun games that will allow him to express himself, or say something. One example is the game "Use the Last Word." This is a perfect game during family gatherings.

Steps for the "Use the Last Word" game:

1. Choose the person who goes first by drawing lots.

2. Decide upon the type of "punishment" the loser will receive.

3. The first player begins a sentence and ends with a "hanging word."

4. The next player in line will use the "hanging word" to start a new sentence of his own.

5. The next new sentences should always start with the last "hanging word."

6. This goes on until a player is not able to use the "hanging word" in a sentence

7. He is then given a "punishment" that the players have agreed upon prior to starting the game.

8. Each player must consider the capability of the child with the speech problem and should use appropriate "hanging words."

9. Rewards may be given to the winners, including the child with the speech disorder.

Another variation of this game is to sing the last word. Instead of saying it, the players can sing the "hanging word." Singing a song may be more enjoyable, but will reduce the phonetic value of the game.

Picture cards

Cut out pictures of items or places that are present inside your home. You can laminate the cards so they last longer. Next, ask your child to identify the picture by pronouncing the words associated with it. This will teach your child the process of association when he associates the pictures with the objects or places they refer to. You can go around the house with him, pointing at the object and the picture while pronouncing the word clearly. Then tape them on the specific items or places.

Board games

Board games can encourage your child to speak, especially if you converse with him while playing. You should not only play, but you should also start a conversation. This may be about the game or some related topic. Choose an interesting board game that he will enjoy. Word games, such as Boggle, Bookworm or scrabble are ideal.

You can articulate the words as you compose them. Understandably, you will have to use simple words that suit the age and comprehension of your child. Your goal is to let him learn the pronunciation of certain words and to become familiar with new terms.

Building blocks

This is useful for young children ages 5 to 6. You can buy building blocks with the letters of the alphabet and instruct your child to arrange them alphabetically. Then let him read the alphabets out loud. You can gently correct him if he makes a mistake. Never focus on his mistakes because this can worsen his speech problem.

Steps for the building blocks game:

1. Choose a safe and clean area in your house. Place rubber mats on the floor to reduce the risk of injury. You can use his playroom if he has one.

2. Shuffle the alphabet blocks around in his play area.

3. Instruct him to arrange the alphabet blocks according to the alphabetical arrangement of the alphabet song.

4. Give him 30 minutes to finish the task.

5. After 30 minutes, check his arrangement by letting him point to each letter and read or sing it aloud. Correct any mistake he has made in the arrangement or pronunciation of the letters.

6. Once he has passed that stage successfully, ask him to form words using the alphabet blocks. Reward him for every correct word he has arranged and pronounced. The reward can be a piece of his favorite toy set or puzzle. You know his interests and hobbies; so, base your rewards on them.

Plays

Your kid can create one-act plays that he can direct and present to an audience. But he has to play a role and say lines that suit his speech capability. This can be stressful to him because he may have stage fright. Only proceed with this activity if your child agrees to participate and is comfortable with the idea. It's your responsibility to motivate him. If he doesn't agree, then there are still hundreds of other activities you can do at home.

He can also come up with a puppet shows that he and other children can enjoy. The idea is for your child to have fun while learning simultaneously.

Flashcards

You can use alphabet flash cards to focus on your child's phonetic disorder. There are plenty of cheap and attractive flash cards that you can buy from bookstores. Another option is to download and print cards from online apps. You can do this activity at home during weekends or mornings when your child is still in his playful mood. Flash cards with a letter and an image are preferable because your child can associate the letter with the image.

Steps for the flash card game:

1. Let your child sit in a comfortable and secure position.

2. Stay in front of your child, at least two feet away from him.

3. Show the flashcards one by one in alphabetical order starting with letter "A". The cards must be at eye level with your child, and the letters must be big enough for him to read.

4. Let your child read the letter twice, by reading the printed letter once and then repeating it after pointing to and naming the image.

5. If your child makes a mistake when reading the letter, you have to correct him by pronouncing it correctly. You can then instruct your child to repeat after you.

6. Proceed to the other letters until he successfully articulates all of them.

7. Take a break if your child shows signs of exhaustion. You can always continue when he is able to absorb the lesson well. Don't force him to continue if he doesn't want to, as this will only fuel his disinterest. Your child can only learn if he's interested in the lesson.

Guessing game

Let your child guess the name of the items through pictures of them. Prepare pictures of common things he encounters every day, such as items inside the house (tables, beds, chairs, etc.), items on the street (cars, signposts, bus stops, etc.), or even items inside a market (fruits, vegetables, eggs, etc.).

Show him the picture and let him name the item. You can let him name ten pictures first, allowing him to master them, before proceeding with the next items. Remember, it's not quantity but quality that counts. He may be able to name a few but if he remembers them correctly, then that will be more reliable than for him to memorize everything but then forgetting them in the long run.

Watching, Listening and Re-enacting

This is an activity that involves your television (TV). There are children's programs featured on certain channels that your child could watch, listen to and then re-enact. One example is Big Bird's TV programs. You can videotape the program and allow your child to watch and re-enact it. Instruct him to write down notes, so he can remember the lines and words. After he performs, inform him of the things he missed and let him re-enact it again.

His re-enactment should include the correct intonation and diction presented in the program.

Cleaning the bedroom

You can let your child clean up his own bedroom. While cleaning, ask him to name the different items he has tidied up. Again, this is killing two birds with one stone. Devise your activities in such a way that you can accomplish two or more goals after the task.

Bathing

With a little imagination, your child can learn while taking a bath. He can name the items inside the bathroom as he uses them. Be alert to correct errors in intonation, pronunciation and accents. Examples of these terms are soap, shower, towel and water. You can also use verbs or action words, such as wash, dry, hang, float, rinse and scrub.

Touring

You can tour locally or internationally with your kid. Teach your child to name the different things that you encounter along the way. Naturally, you have to use only one language, preferably English, so as not to confuse your child. Enjoy your time conversing with your child as you improve his skills in speech and articulation, eliminating his phonological disorder.

Imagination games

Let your child draw any object or scene using his imagination. Let him describe the meaning of his drawing in clear and concise words. He can also create and direct imaginary characters and assign dialogues to enliven his characters. With the help of his friends, he can learn how to express himself and explore his creativeness.

Blowing Bubbles

You can also blow bubbles with your kid to exercise his lips and make them more flexible in forming words. There are commercially prepared Blow Bubbles toys that you can easily purchase at your nearest toy store.

Reading Books

This is a technique that is helpful for both adults and children. When children read books out loud it helps in improving their phonological disorder. You child can read any kind of book that he wants but poems and rhymes are extremely effective. It's better to make him read books that would actually interest him rather than making him read something that wouldn't interest him. Kids love fantasy books, short stories and other similar books.

Reading also helps in developing intellectual skills especially in kids, so you can help you child with his speech disorder while at the same time helping him learn more.

You can correct any mistakes he makes, so he can improve his speech more. However, do so with tact—don't give your child the impression that all you do is focus on his mistakes or that you are disappointed with him. In other words, praise his efforts and ensure that you child is motivated and the exercises remain fun. Don't make them too long, humorless or forced.

Adding words

This is a phonetic exercise. Your child starts with one word and then you add more words to it. Repeat the same procedure anew, but this time, say one word and ask him to add more words to it.

Here's an example:

He says "bed"

You add "room" to produce the word "bedroom"

He says "Roses"

You add "bouquet of" to produce "bouquet of roses"

You can gradually expand the words into phrases until the exercise boosts his mental alertness and vocabulary. Reverse the roles and motivate him to think of precise words that are well pronounced. Remember to teach him how to properly enunciate the words.

Licking Ice Cream

Place a sufficient amount of ice cream on your child's lips and allow him to lick it slowly with his tongue. While he licks, he should feel his tongue twist and turn, and his lips adjust to the movement of his tongue. This will help exercise his lips, palate and tongue.

It is an unconventional technique but it's still pretty helpful and your kid would do it willingly just to eat some ice cream.

Chapter 3: Strategies for Adults

Adults can have speech impairment too - you ought to know this fact because it's important. There are a number of causes why adults can have this disorder too. The reasons include aphasia (blood clot in the brain), vocal impairment (injury to the vocal cord, mouth or palate), spasmodic dysphonia (the involuntary movements of the vocal cord), and dysarthria (weak vocal muscles).

There are also instances when adults have speech impairment during myocardial infarctions (heart attacks) and cerebrovascular accidents (strokes). Hence, sudden adult speech impairment can denote a serious condition, which must prompt immediate medical attention.

To allow you to have a variety of methods to select from, here are some more speech therapy exercises you can choose. The duration, intensity and frequency of the exercises can affect the results. The protocol is to perform the exercises at least twice daily for 20 minutes to one hour.

Mirror exercises

Use the mirror and ask your friend or family member to demonstrate to you the appearance of the mouth when pronouncing words properly. You can mimic the actions as both of you stand before the mirror. This will exercise the oral cavity as well.

Drinking liquids through a straw

This is another excellent exercise to improve your oral motor function. Sucking on a straw will purse the lips and will increase the flexibility of your mouth.

Reading books

Reading books out loud can help improve your phonetics and eliminate your phonological disorder. You can read rhymes or poems that you can readily relate to. Ask another person to correct any mistakes that you make, so you can improve your speech more.

Chewing gum

The simple act of chewing gum can serve as a mouth-strengthening exercise that can significantly improve your speech disorder. Chewing strengthens the muscles of the mouth and jaw. These body parts are important in speech.

Playing the harmonica

When you blow on the harmonica or play other wind instruments, you will exercise your lips and mouth. This can aid in the correct enunciation of the words, and exercise your oral muscles.

Pressing the tongue

This is a superb oral motor exercise. This is how it's done.

Steps:

1. Stick out your tongue.

2. Press a tongue depressor against it.

3. Push hard against the tongue depressor.

4. Hold the action for 6 seconds.

5. After 6 seconds, relax your tongue.

6. Repeat this at least 6 to 7 times.

7. Do the same exercise by sticking out the right side of your tongue and press against it.

8. Proceed to the left side of your tongue and perform the same steps.

You can do this twice daily, once in the morning and once in the evening.

Whistling

Whistling is fun and also very simple. If you don't how to do it then you learn from a friend or watch some YouTube videos. This will exercise your vocal cords and other parts of his mouth.

Humming with a candy in the mouth

The great Greek orator, Demosthenes, once had a speech disorder, and he successfully corrected this by placing pebbles in his mouth. Who knows? You may be able to correct your speech disorder too through this unconventional method. This technique exercises your speech function and the muscles along the vocal cords. A well-toned vocal muscle will help produce perfect sounds.

All of these are really simple techniques; hence many people tend to underestimate their usefulness and effectiveness in treating speech disorders. They can be performed easily at home without much effort hence they are perfect for adults. Most adults don't really have the time to perform complicated speech therapy techniques hence these techniques have been designed to be time effective.

Chapter 4: Therapy for Speech Disorders

There are methods applied to people with speech disorders with the purpose of improving their condition. These therapeutic interventions are based on the cause of the speech disorder. The underlying cause has to be treated so that the speech disorder can be eliminated or reduced. Here are recommended methods for the following causes:

Autism or ASD

For ASD, the management is similar to the activities recommended for simple speech disorders. Speech, language and occupational therapy are needed to manage ASD. Emphasis is on the management of the behavior of autistic persons because this is typically the cause of their speech disorders. When autism is dealt with, the speech problem will eventually disappear.

Apraxia or CAS

The intervention applied here is occupational or physical therapy. Your child will be subjected to oral muscle exercises that can promote proper coordination of his muscles and his vocal cords.

Intellectual disability

The method applied to remedy this condition is for your child to undergo a complete assessment that includes diagnostic laboratory tests to exclude hormonal problems such as cretinism, hypothyroidism or dwarfism resulting from insufficient Growth Hormones (GH). After the lab results are evaluated and the results confirm insufficient thyroid hormones (TH) or GH, suitable medications will be given to correct the hormonal insufficiency.

Hypothyroidism requires iodine or synthetic preparations of Triiodothyronine (T3) and Thyroxine (T4) as oral treatments. For GH, oral or synthetic preparations of GH can also be used to treat the lack of these hormones. However, these medications should be prescribed by a doctor because they are not ordinary medications. If taken incorrectly, they can cause serious conditions, such as hyperthyroidism or gigantism.

These are conditions caused by elevated levels of these hormones in the bloodstream. Therefore, a health specialist must be consulted before taking any of these medications. Examples of hypothyroid treatments are unithroid oral, Levothyroxine oral, and Triostat intravenous. Examples of GH insufficiency medications are recombinant human growth hormone (rHGH).

Neurological conditions

For treatment of neurological conditions, you have to first consult a neurologist. This specialist will find out the specific neurologic condition that is causing a problem.

Interventions commonly involve physical and occupational therapy. Angiography Interventions can also be applied, whenever necessary.

Auditory processing disorder (APD)

This condition requires the evaluation of the auditory canal and then treatment for the damaged part of the organ. APD interventions may involve speech-language and audio logic approaches. These are similar to the methods used for children suffering from ADHD. The key factor is to be aware that auditory processing is dependent upon many factors, such as reading, neurophysiology, cognition, language, memory and visualization. Therefore, the treatment needed involves multiple strategies.

Selective mutism

This is a behavioral disorder, so it can be treated by changing behavior. It's not something that someone is born with but it's something that people develop due to many reasons. If you had a traumatic incident then it is entirely possible that you can't seem to speak in certain situations that remind you of that trauma.

The best way to deal with this is to solve the problem from the root. Understand why the selective mutism developed and try to talk about the trauma in order to solve the reaction that it has on speech. Another technique is to stay away from such incidents so that the trauma never resurfaces.

Hearing loss

A hearing test has to be conducted to confirm the hearing loss. This is done through physical and sound tests. Treatment can commence based on the final findings. If the hearing loss is due to earwax accumulation, the effective treatment is to remove the earwax by using warm saline water (salt water) or hydrogen peroxide.

For adults, it is recommended to go to a specialist instead of asking someone else to clear the earwax for you.

Steps for removing accumulated earwax:

1. Let your child sit in a comfortable position and tilt the ear with the accumulated earwax upwards.

2. Using a cotton pad/ball, allow it to absorb the saline water.

3. Squeeze the cotton pad/ball and allow 2 to 3 drops to fall inside your child's ear. Allow some time for the saline water to reach the earwax.

4. Tilt his head the opposite side to allow his ear with the earwax drain.

5. Do this several times until the earwax loosens up and comes out of his ear.

6. The elimination of the earwax will allow your child to hear properly.

If the hearing loss is due to a damaged ear canal or eardrum, then your health specialist may resort to surgical intervention or treatment.

Defects of speech organs

Defects in the speech organs, such as a harelip or damaged vocal cords can cause speech problems. The method applicable in these cases is surgical intervention. Medications won't be able to cure a harelip or injured vocal cord.

For each specific condition, an appropriate treatment is applied. There are similar therapeutic interventions for most of the conditions because they all deal with speech impairment or disorder.

Chapter 5: Increasing Effectiveness

Aside from adopting the exercises provided in this book, it's vital to observe the following tips when implementing the speech therapy exercises. This will ensure that the exercises are effective. These tips can be followed by both adults and kids.

➤ Be ingenious. You can create your own activities based on your preferences. The more fun your activity is, the better.

➤ Ascertain that there are no serious underlying conditions before starting your exercises. No matter what you do, if there is a disease that is causing the problem, you can never overcome your speech disorder. You have to treat the root cause before relying on speech therapy exercises.

➤ The progress must be regularly evaluated. This will allow you to know if the methods/interventions are successful or not. If they're not, you can change the treatment and utilize other strategies until you achieve your desired results. Don't change the method immediately though. Allow sufficient time for the method to take effect.

➤ A child's personality can affect his treatment. Since speech is part of a child's behavior, his personal traits will certainly affect the success of his treatment. You cannot use musical instrument exercises with a child who dislikes music unless you motivate him to like music.

➤ There's no one specific method that can be effective in all speech disorder cases. Individual differences, behavior, and the cause of the speech disorder affect the success of the therapeutic intervention.

➢ After each intervention, a report should be written and documented. This is a protocol that you have to remember to ensure that your efforts are not useless.

➢ The goal of each exercise must be clearly identified. This is so that you can readily ascertain whether the goal has been achieved or not, by simply checking the results.

➢ There has to be a coordination of efforts from everyone concerned about the treatment. Everyone should be willing to share his or her expertise in contributing positively to the progress of the treatment.

➢ Great listening skills are important in good speech. You should emphasize to your child that he can only speak well if he is a good listener.

➢ A speech/language pathologist is the best health specialist. This is the most recommended specialist for people with speech disorders.

➢ Encourage all family members and friends to speak properly. This will help in demonstrating proper speech to your child with speech disorder.

➢ Enlisting the help of a teacher can help. You can have a chat with your child's teacher so that your home exercises will complement and enhance his school activities.

➢ Be a role model in speech. Speak clearly and distinctly for your child to emulate. Enunciate properly and follow correct diction. Show by example what proper speech is all about.

> Develop your child's vocabulary by introducing new words regularly. You can do this during his daily speech exercises. Don't flood him with new words though, because if he is "drowned", he might shut down automatically, and not be able to remember anything.

> As an adult, it's important to not feel disheartened due to societal pressure. Remember that it is common for many adults to have a speech disorder and it isn't something that is exclusively impacting you.

Conclusion

Speech Therapy can only be effective if it is performed with the right kind of mindset and patience. Forcing therapy on anyone never works unless the person himself desires to change. So, all the exercises in this book will be useless unless they are performed with a positive mindset and you don't expect immediate results.

All the exercises in this book have one thing in common – they aren't specialized but mostly in the paradigm of home remedies. Performing them doesn't require a lot of effort but that shouldn't make you complacent. You should continue to practice regularly to ensure best results.

Thank you for buying this book and I hope that it was helpful!

And finally, if you liked the book, I would like to ask you to do me a favor and leave a review for the book on Amazon – it will barely take you 40 seconds.

Thank you and good luck!

Made in the USA
Coppell, TX
08 July 2020